THE VERY CLEVER CONSONANT BLENDS

PHONICS READ-ALOUDS

Title: The Very Clever Consonant Blends
ISBN: 9798300843977
First Published in the United States of America, 2024

Contributors: Manns, Yvette, author; Blu, Ana K., illustrator

Summary: After a fun day at the beach, the consonants go on a quest to help their friend Sly save his smoothie store. They meet a new friend that teaches them how to blend their sounds at the beginning of words.

www.PhonicsReadAlouds.com

THE VERY CLEVER CONSONANT BLENDS

Written by: Yvette Manns
Illustrated by: Ana K. Blu

It was a bright spring morning, with only a few clouds in the sky. The consonants were playing water sports at Consonant Cove. Some letters were swimming, others were snorkeling, and the rest were waterskiing.

By the afternoon, they were ready for a break. "We should grab a sweet treat," R remarked. S suggested, "How about something healthy, like a smoothie?" L replied, "Let's do it!"

The consonants dried off and skipped down the street to their favorite smoothie place. “I can’t wait to get an extra large green smoothie!” G exclaimed.

When they entered the store, Sly, the owner, glanced up and gave them a slight wave. He usually greeted them with a big smile, but today, Sly slumped on his stool. G asked, "Why so glum, Sly?"

"I have a major problem," Sly cried. "My freezer was left open all night, and my fruit spoiled! I can't spend any more money this week because I just bought this special blender."

“How will we order our smoothies?” W wondered aloud. Sly shrugged and said, “Sorry, Consonants. I’m going to have to close down the store for the day. You all can hang out here as long as you want. Just lock the door when you leave.”

"Poor Sly," S sighed. "I wish we could help him." Suddenly, the blender said, "Hi, I'm Blendy! I can create anything you want! Just add the ingredients to my container!"
B asked, "Can we add any ingredient?"
"Yes!" Blendy answered.

Perplexed, P asked B, “What are you blabbing about?” B beamed. “Blendy explained how to make new things! Do you know how we put our sounds together to create words? What if we could put our sounds together in Blendy instead? Maybe we could build new words, and those words might be able to create fruit for the store. Let’s try it!”

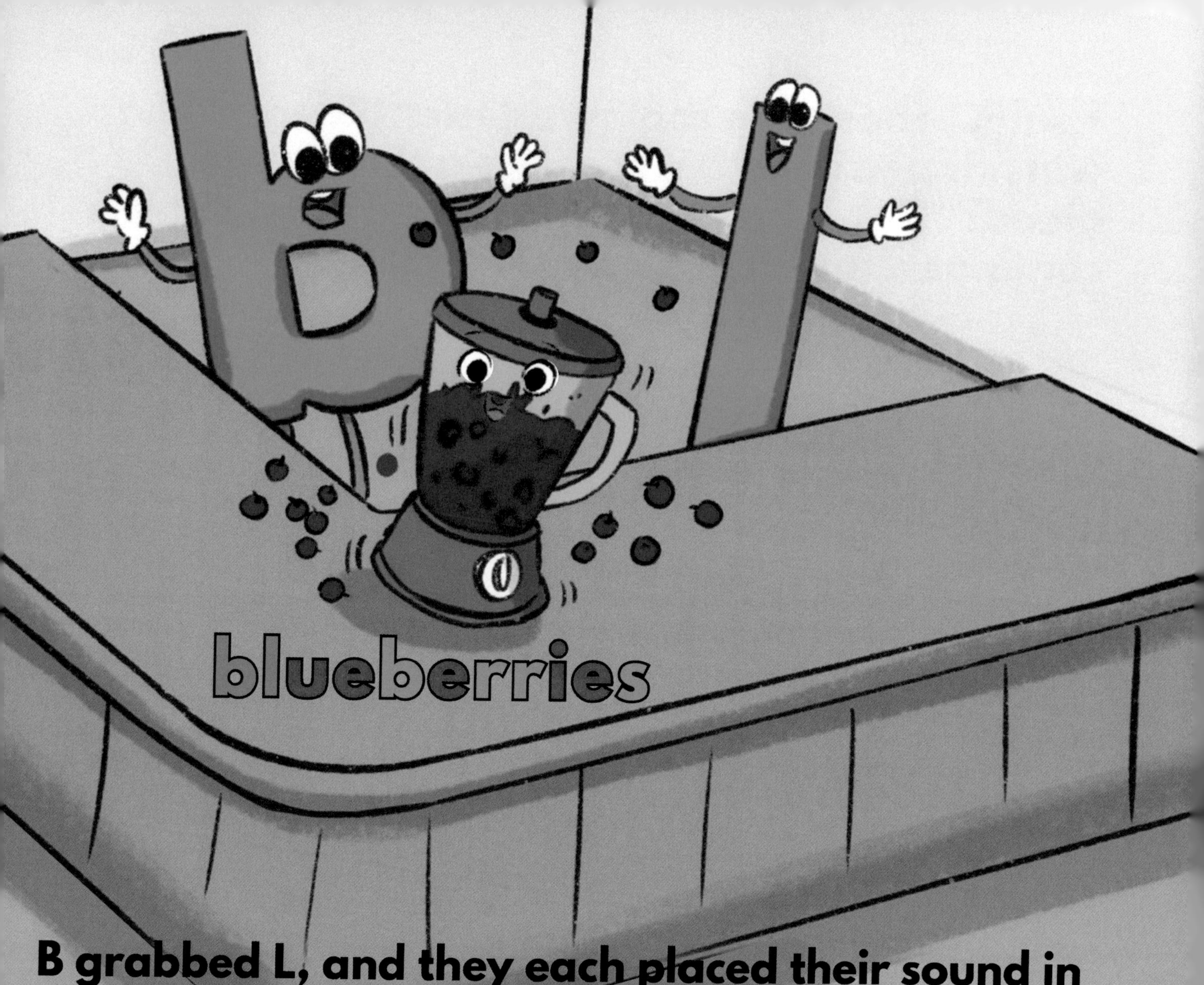

B grabbed L, and they each placed their sound in the container. B opened the lid of the blender, and inside were fresh blueberries! “Wow!” B bellowed. “We created a word with more than one consonant at the beginning, and we each kept our own sounds!”

T said, "Those are cool two-letter blends! What will happen if we try to make a three-letter blend?" S, T, and R put their sounds in Blendy's container, and strawberries appeared!

strawberries

S said, “When two or three of us are next to each other at the beginning of a word or syllable, we can still hear our individual sounds. Friends, I think we just created consonant blends!”

Just then, Sly appeared in the doorway. “Hey, Consonants, I forgot to tell you—”
Sly’s mouth dropped open, and he blinked his eyes in disbelief. “We created consonant blends in your special blender,” F explained. “Watch this!” F grabbed R, and they placed their sounds inside. Different kinds of fruits blasted out of the blender!

Sly clapped his hands. "You all are brilliant! Now I can provide even more smoothie flavors than ever before. Let's go tell your vowel friends what you've created. They'll be so pleased!"

Sly and the consonants ran to Vowel Valley to tell A, E, I, O, and U their exciting news. B blared, “We just discovered consonant blends that come at the beginning of words! Come build words with us!” B and R built the word brag, T and W built the word twin, and S, P, and L built the word split.

A asked, “Since you all are putting your sounds in Blendy’s container to make consonant blends, does this mean you are mixing your sounds together to make a new sound?”

"No," Sly responded. "Each consonant keeps their own sound, so their color never changes in the new words." B added, "That's right! Our colors stay blue. Speaking of 'blue,' you can hear both the /b/ sound and the /l/ sound at the beginning of the word."

"Well, Sly," B said. "Blendy helped us discover consonant blends. Now you can create new smoothie flavors, and we can help learners spell and read words with consonant blends at the beginning. How does that make you feel?"

"GROOVY!"
Sly shouted.

TIPS FOR AFTER READING

- Go on a word hunt and list all the words in this story with consonant blends at the beginning.
- Sort the words you find by the beginning blend pattern and share with a classmate.
- Read all the words with consonant blends at the beginning out loud.
- Draw Blendy and list as many consonant blends as you can.
- Using another passage or text, highlight all the words with consonant blends at the beginning that you can find.

FUN FACTS ABOUT
INITIAL CONSONANT BLENDS

- Initial consonant blends are two or three consonants that are at the beginning of a syllable or a word.
- When you read words with initial consonant blends, you hear all the sounds represented by the letters.
- Blends are different from digraphs. Blends keep their own letter sounds and digraphs create one new sound.
- Sometimes blends are sorted into categories of L-blends, R-blends, and S-blends so we can learn a few at a time.
- Only certain combinations of two and three letters can create a consonant blend. For example, "bx" is not a consonant blend, but "bl" is a consonant blend.
- When you are mapping words that have an initial consonant blend, each letter gets its own box.
- Here are some more words that begin with consonant blends:

block bring clap crab drop flag frog glad
grow plants scrub slide spray stop street trip

CAN YOU THINK OF ANY MORE WORDS WITH INITIAL CONSONANT BLENDS?

CHECK OUT OTHER BOOKS IN THE SERIES!

...and more books!

STAY IN THE KNOW!

Visit www.PhonicsReadAlouds.com for activities, stickers, and more!

DID YOU ENJOY THIS STORY?

Please consider leaving us a review on Amazon. This helps us to learn what you want to read about next and tell other people about our stories!

PhonicsReadAlouds PhonicsReadAlouds PhonicsReadAlouds

Made in the USA
Monee, IL
12 December 2024

73498916R00017